THE
LOOK AND SEE
BIBLE

Sally Ann Wright

Illustrated by Moira Maclean

CONTENTS

A BEAUTIFUL WORLD

At the beginning of time, God made a beautiful world.

God made light to shine in the darkness. He made the sky above and the sea below. God made dry land and filled it with tall trees and blossoms and flowering plants.

God filled the heavens with sun and moon, stars and planets.

God filled the seas and rivers with fish, large and small, and the sky with birds of every size and color.

God put animals in the fields and animals in the woods. He made them patterned and striped, with tusks and with tails. God made a man and a woman to be his friends. He walked and talked with them and gave them all they needed to be happy.

And God was pleased with all he had made.

Look and see how many birds there are in the sky.

NOAH AND THE GREAT FLOOD

Noah was a good man. He loved God and wanted to please him.

But the world was no longer the wonderful place God had made. The people cared only about themselves. They fought and stole and hurt each other.

God was sad. He decided to send a great flood to wash the earth clean again.

God told Noah to build a boat to float on the flood waters. Inside the boat Noah put two of every kind of animal under the sun: elephants and rhinos, cats and crocodiles, lions and leopards, monkeys and tiny mice.

Then the rain came. For forty long days and nights it rained, until the earth was covered with water. But Noah, his family, and the animals were all kept safe.

When the water went down and dry land appeared, Noah let all the creatures run wild again. Noah thanked God for looking after them. And God put a beautiful rainbow in the sky.

Look and see which colors in the rainbow you can name.

GOD MAKES A PROMISE

Abraham trusted God.

When God told him to move, Abraham moved. He took his wife and servants, his sheep, goats, and camels, and camped in tents until God told him where to make a new home in the land of Canaan.

When God told him he would have a large family, Abraham waited for it to happen – even when he had to wait a very long time.

"You will have children," promised God. "And your children will have children. And your grandchildren will have children – until there are more people in your family than there are stars in the sky or grains of sand on the beach!"

Abraham was old. His wife, Sarah, was old. He had many sheep and goats but he did not have a son.

Then many years later, Sarah had a baby boy. They called him Isaac, which meant "laughter."

Look and see how many stars are in the sky.

A SPECIAL WIFE FOR ISAAC

Abraham's son, Isaac, was soon a grown man. Abraham wanted him to have a wife who loved him and who loved the one true God, so Abraham sent a servant to his homeland.

The servant traveled a long way until he stopped by a well with his ten thirsty camels. Then he prayed. He asked God to show him the right wife for Isaac. The woman who showed her kindness to strangers by offering to bring water for him and his camels would be the right one.

Rebecca was fetching water at the well that day. She offered the servant a drink and then she brought water for the camels – all ten of them!

Then the servant went to Rebecca's house, where he found that she was part of Abraham's family. She agreed to go back with him to be Isaac's wife.

Isaac knew at once Rebecca was special, and he loved her.

Look and see which man is Abraham's servant.

12

THE BROTHERS WHO QUARRELED

Esau and Jacob were Isaac and Rebecca's twin sons. Like boys in every family, they were quite different from each other and sometimes quarreled!

Esau grew up to be a hairy man; he liked to hunt. Jacob had smooth skin; he liked to cook..

When Isaac was an old man, he asked Esau, the twin born first, to go out hunting so Isaac could have a tasty meal. Then he would bless him.

Rebecca heard what Isaac said. She wanted Isaac to bless Jacob instead. So she told him to play a trick on his father.

Isaac could no longer see very well. Rebecca put goatskins on Jacob so that when Isaac touched him, he felt hairy like Esau. The trick worked. Isaac thought Jacob was Esau – and Jacob got his father's blessing.

Esau was very angry. Jacob was so afraid, he ran away to live with his uncle. It was many years before the brothers met again, but when they did, Jacob was sorry and the brothers made up.

Look and see Esau the hunter.

THE FAVORITE SON

Jacob had been Rebecca's favorite son. When Jacob had children of his own, Joseph was his favorite.

To show Joseph that he loved him, Jacob gave him a beautiful long-sleeved coat.

Then Joseph started to have strange dreams. He told his brothers that one day he would be so important that they would have to bow down to him.

This made the brothers not only jealous, but angry too. They plotted to kill him...but then realized that instead they could sell him to some traders, who would take him away to Egypt.

But God had plans for Joseph and his family. First Joseph's dreams came true, and he became an important ruler in Egypt.

Then, years later, when there was no food in Jacob's land, the brothers went to Egypt. When the brothers asked for help, Joseph was able to give them food and help them all make their home with him.

Look and see Jacob's only daughter.

THE PRINCESS AND THE BABY

After Joseph died, the king of Egypt made the Israelite people his slaves, and he made them work very hard. But there were many Israelites, and he was afraid that one day they would fight him. So the king decided that all baby boys should be killed.

But when baby Moses was born, his mother wouldn't let the soldiers take him away. She made a special basket, put her baby inside, and hid it near the riverbank. Miriam, Moses' big sister, watched nearby.

Soon the princess came down to the river. She saw the basket and heard a baby crying. When she looked inside, she found baby Moses and wanted to keep him!

Miriam went to the princess and told her that her mother would look after the baby. And so Moses was kept safe. When he was big enough, he went to live in the palace.

God had great plans for Moses. One day he would lead God's people out of Egypt into the promised land of Canaan.

Look and see how many women there are.

THE WALLS THAT TUMBLED DOWN

Moses died in the desert after watching over God's people for many years. Then God asked Joshua to lead his people to a wonderful new land.

Joshua took the people across the River Jordan. But when they reached the city of Jericho, they were frightened. The city had strong, high walls, and inside the city were fierce, unfriendly people.

How could God's people get through the city?

God told Joshua that they must march around the walls for six days while the priests blew on trumpets. On the seventh day, they must march around the city not once, not twice, but seven times!

So the people did as Joshua told them. When the priests blew their trumpets...and all the people shouted...the walls of the city crashed to the ground!

The promised land was theirs. After years of slavery in Egypt and more years wandering in the desert, God's people had a home in the land of Canaan.

Look and see the walls crashing down.

DEBORAH LEADS HER PEOPLE

God's people lived in Canaan for many years, but they found it hard to live by the rules God had given them. Sometimes they married people from the other tribes; sometimes they worshipped the false gods of those around them.

After Joshua died, God sent wise judges to help them live the right way. One of these was Deborah.

God's people came to Deborah and told her how they hated Jabin, the cruel king of the land, and his army chief, Sisera. Then God told Deborah how to free his people.

Deborah told Barak to lead the army against King Jabin. But Barak was afraid. He said he would go only if Deborah would go with him.

So they went to Mount Tabor together, and with their small army they charged down on Sisera and his 900 iron chariots. Then God sent down rain.

Sisera's chariots got stuck in the mud and Barak's soldiers were able to win the battle. God's people were free!

Look and see how many horses there are.

GIDEON TRUSTS GOD

Time passed and God's people forgot once more how he had helped them.

Then a new enemy came. The Midianites stole their grain so they couldn't make bread; they stole their grapes and olives, their sheep and goats. At last God's people asked him for help.

God did not choose a brave soldier. God chose a shy man called Gideon, who would listen to him and trust him.

Gideon chose 300 soldiers to help him. He gave them all a trumpet and a burning torch inside a jar.

Gideon waited until it was dark and told his men to surround the camp of the Midianites. Then he blew his trumpet, and all his soldiers copied him. They all broke their jars on the ground and shouted.

The enemy was so frightened and confused that the Midianites started to fight each other. Then they ran away into the darkness.

God had answered his people. Their enemy had gone.

Look and see the broken pots.

SAMSON, THE STRONG MAN

God chose Samson to defend his people against the cruel Philistines. Samson had never had his hair cut because he knew that this was the sign of the huge strength God had given him.

The Philistines wanted to know Samson's secret. So they paid Delilah to find out.

Delilah asked Samson about his strength again and again and again. At first he tricked her when she asked. But finally he gave in and told her his secret. Then, when Samson was asleep, the Philistines cut off his hair. They blinded Samson and put him in chains. Samson was no longer God's strong man.

But God gave Samson another chance. Now that the Philistines were no longer afraid, they brought Samson out from the prison to laugh at him. But God gave him back his strength one last time. Samson pushed down the pillars of their temple, and died while destroying thousands of God's enemies.

Look and see what color belt Samson is wearing.

THE BOY WHO LISTENED

Hannah had always wanted a baby. When God answered her prayer she thanked him by letting her little boy, Samuel, serve him in the temple. Samuel went to help Eli, the priest, and he learned to love God.

One night, Samuel went to bed as usual.

He was woken by a voice calling his name.

Samuel got up and ran to Eli.

"Here I am!" he said.

"But I didn't call you," said Eli. "Go back to bed."

Samuel went back to bed, but soon he heard his name again. Samuel got up and rushed back to Eli.

"Here I am!" he said.

When this happened for the third time, Eli was puzzled. Then he wondered whether it could be God who was calling Samuel.

"If it happens again," Eli told Samuel, "say: 'Speak, Lord, I am listening.'"

Samuel did as he was told, and God did speak to him. Samuel listened, and from that time on, he showed God's people the right way to live again.

Look and see Samuel's night light.

SAUL AND THE MISSING DONKEYS

One day, Saul's father, Kish, told him their donkeys were missing. He sent Saul with a servant to try to find them.

Saul and the servant looked for two days, but they couldn't find the missing donkeys. Then they realized they were near the place where Samuel lived. Perhaps he could help them find the donkeys?

Samuel was now an old man, but he still listened to God. God had told him he would meet Saul and that he, Samuel, must anoint him as the first king of Israel.

Samuel told Saul straight away that his donkeys were safe and that he had an important message from God. But when he told him he would be king, Saul couldn't believe it!

The next day Samuel took him aside and anointed him with oil. This would be a secret until later, when all the people would know that God had chosen Saul to be their king.

Look and see how many donkeys there are in the picture.

DAVID, THE GIANT-KILLER

David was Jesse's youngest son. His older brothers were in King Saul's army, but David looked after his father's sheep.

One day, David went to see his brothers. He watched as the Philistine champion, a giant called Goliath, marched up and down taunting the soldiers.

"Who will come and fight me?" shouted Goliath.

Saul's soldiers were too frightened! No one stepped forward. But David went to King Saul. He offered to fight the giant.

"God saved me from the lion and the bear when I looked after my father's sheep," he said. "God will help me now."

Saul was amazed! He offered David his armor and weapons but they were too big and heavy. Instead David took five smooth pebbles from the stream and whirled one around in his sling. The stone hit Goliath on the forehead and he fell down dead!

All the soldiers cheered! David had trusted God and God had helped him defeat the giant.

Look and see which animals are watching David.

SOLOMON, THE WISE KING

David became king after Saul, and David's son,
Solomon, became king after his father. One
night Solomon dreamed that God was asking
him a question.

"What gift shall I give you?" God asked.

If he wanted, Solomon could have chosen to
be rich or famous or happy...

"Help me to be a wise king," he answered.

So God made him very wise. One day two
women came because they were arguing over
a baby.

"It's mine!" said one mother.

"No, her baby died," said the other. "This
baby is mine!"

Solomon told his guard to bring a sword and
divide the baby in half. At this the real mother
offered to give the baby away rather than
have the child die. So Solomon gave the child to
its real mother.

But God also made Solomon rich and famous.
Solomon built a magnificent temple with his
money, a special place where people could pray
and worship God.

Look and see how many camels there are.

ELIJAH RUNS FROM KING AHAB

Not all the kings loved God as Solomon did. Ahab was a bad king. He didn't listen to God and he worshipped the false god Baal.

God sent Elijah to Ahab with a message: soon there would be no more rain. Unless Ahab changed his ways, all the water in the rivers would dry up, and everything would die.

Ahab was furious! Elijah feared for his life and ran away to hide in the Kerith Ravine. There God sent ravens to feed him, and he could drink water from the stream.

Then God sent Elijah to a poor widow who shared her food with him and her son. For as long as she shared with Elijah, her jar of flour and jug of oil never ran out.

When Elijah went back to see the king, he challenged all the people to choose to serve the one true God again. This was the only God who could send both fire and rain.

Look and see how many ravens there are.

NAAMAN WASHES IN THE RIVER

Elisha had learned from Elijah how to listen to God. Soon he was able to take God's messages to his people.

In Syria there was a servant girl who came from Israel and knew all about Elisha. Naaman, her master, was a commander in the army. The girl watched as her master became more and more ill. He had a horrible skin disease and no doctor could make him better.

"I wish he could go to Elisha," she told her mistress. "God gives him power to make people well again."

So Naaman traveled to Israel to find Elisha and ask for help. Elisha sent Naaman a message:

"Wash seven times in the River Jordan. You will be healed."

But Naaman expected more than this. Surely Syria had better rivers than Israel! But Naaman washed in the river as he was told, and his skin was made clean and new again. The little servant girl was right.

Look and see the children playing in the river.

THE ANGEL OF DEATH

Hezekiah was a good king. He loved God and was kind to his people.

But Sennacherib, the wicked king of Assyria, tried to invade his land. At first Hezekiah begged him to leave and paid him silver and gold. Sennacherib took the money but still brought a large army to attack Hezekiah. He surrounded the city with his men and stopped them from getting any food. It would not be long before Hezekiah and all his people would starve to death.

Hezekiah trusted God. He told his people not to be afraid and asked God to help them.

Sennacherib laughed at Hezekiah and told the people not to believe him.

"Your God won't help you!" he shouted.

But Hezekiah asked the prophet Isaiah to pray too. God heard their prayers and sent an angel to protect them. In the morning, Sennacherib's whole army lay dead.

Then Sennacherib realized that Hezekiah's God was real and he ran away. God's people were saved.

Look and see King Hezekiah.

JONAH RUNS FROM GOD

God sent Jonah to tell the people of Nineveh that they needed to change their ways. They were cruel and wicked. But Jonah didn't want to! He jumped aboard a ship and ran away.

Soon the wind blew in the sails and the waves crashed against the sides. The sailors feared for their lives.

Jonah knew that God had found him!

"Throw me into the sea and the storm will stop raging!" he told the sailors.

So they threw Jonah overboard where he was swallowed by a big fish. Jonah stayed inside the fish for three days and three nights.

Jonah told God he was wrong to run away and was sorry. And the fish spat him out on a beach.

Then Jonah went to Nineveh and talked to the people there. They listened to him and were sorry. They promised to change their ways. And God forgave them.

Look and see the big tail of the fish.

DANIEL IS THROWN TO THE LIONS

During the time of King Zedekiah, the Babylonians destroyed Jerusalem. They took away many of the people to work for them. One of these was Daniel.

Daniel served King Darius in Babylon. He prayed to God every day, but he also worked very hard so that the king trusted him and gave him an important job. This made other men jealous. Soon they were plotting against Daniel.

A new rule was made that everyone must pray to the king or be thrown into the lions' den. But Daniel would pray only to God. The king had no choice but to have him thrown to the lions.

The next morning the king went to see what had happened to Daniel.

"Was your God able to keep you safe?" he asked at the door of the den.

"My God closed the mouths of the lions," replied Daniel. "I am still here."

The king was delighted! He made a new rule that everyone should worship Daniel's God.

Look and see how many lions there are.

NEHEMIAH REBUILDS THE WALLS

God's people had been taken away from their home. After many years, they were allowed to return. But the walls of the city of Jerusalem had been pulled down and Solomon's beautiful temple had been destroyed.

The people began to rebuild, but it was hard and took a long time. News reached Nehemiah who was still in Babylon, and he asked if he could go home to rebuild the walls and the gates.

When Nehemiah saw how much work there was to do, he prayed for help and made his plans. He encouraged his friends and ignored the people who laughed at him and said the work couldn't be done.

Nehemiah would not give up.

When the walls were finished, Nehemiah thanked God and asked Ezra to read God's law to the people.

Then they realized how bad they had been and how good God was to forgive them. They were home at last.

Look and see the men with the hammers.

ESTHER SAVES HER PEOPLE

Xerxes, the king of Persia, wanted a wife who was beautiful and loyal. Esther was very beautiful but she was also one of God's people. Yet Xerxes chose Esther to be his queen.

Mordecai, Esther's cousin, also served the king, and had once saved the king's life.

At that time, there was a man called Haman who worked at the palace. He did not like Mordecai because he would not bow to him and worship him. He did not like any of God's people. So he started to plot to have them all killed.

The queen was not supposed to talk to her husband unless he asked her to. But Esther knew she had to save her people if she could. Esther told King Xerxes about Haman's wicked plan.

King Xerxes was so angry with Haman that he gave orders for him to be killed instead.

So Esther, the beautiful queen, saved God's people. And the king rewarded Mordecai for saving his life.

Look and see which man is Mordecai.

THE BABY IN THE MANGER

Many years passed and the Romans came to rule over God's people. They ordered a census to count them all.

Mary and Joseph traveled to Bethlehem to be counted with all the other people whose families were born there. But it was not a good time for Mary. She was expecting her first baby.

Mary's baby was born that night. It was a boy, just as an angel had told her, and she named him Jesus.

Some time later, wise men from the East came to Bethlehem. They had seen a new star in the sky and came to look for a baby king. They followed the star until it stopped over a house.

The wise men brought gifts of gold, frankincense, and myrrh, and they bowed down and worshipped Mary's son.

Mary wondered at these special gifts. Her child was indeed the son of God.

Look and see how many gifts the wise men brought.

JOHN BAPTIZES JESUS

John had been born just before Jesus. God had special plans for him too.

When he was grown up he went into the desert where he wore simple clothes and ate locusts and honey.

Then he came with a message from God for everyone to hear:

"Jesus is coming soon! Listen to what he says and tell God you are sorry for all the wrong things you do."

In the River Jordan John baptized the people who listened to him. Then one day Jesus came to see him.

"Baptize me too, John," said Jesus.

John was surprised. Surely Jesus was too important for John to baptize him! But he did as Jesus asked.

Then John heard God's voice from heaven: "This is my son; I am pleased with him."

The Holy Spirit came like a dove and John knew that Jesus was God's own son. Now it was time for Jesus to start the special work God had given him.

Look and see where Jesus was baptized.

FOLLOWING JESUS

Jesus chose twelve men to be his friends and to go with him wherever he went. He didn't choose them because they were clever or handsome or special in any way. He chose them after asking God about it. Then he asked the men to follow him – and they did.

Peter and Andrew were fishermen.

They were casting their net into the lake when Jesus walked by.

"Come and follow me!" said Jesus. "I will help you catch people instead!"

Peter and Andrew left their nets and followed him. Then Jesus saw James and John.

"Come with me!" said Jesus.

James and John left their nets and followed Jesus, too. Then he chose Philip, Bartholomew, Matthew the tax collector, Thomas the twin, another James, Thaddaeus, Simon, and Judas Iscariot.

All these men chose to follow Jesus when he asked them. From that day on their lives were changed forever.

Look and see how many boats there are.

JESUS GOES TO A WEDDING

Mary was invited to a wedding feast. Jesus and his friends went, too.

At first there was plenty to eat and drink and everyone was having a wonderful time. But after a while, Mary went to Jesus and told him that there was no wine left.

Mary felt certain that God's son could make wonderful things happen. If he wanted to, he could help make sure there was wine enough for everyone.

Jesus asked the servants to fill up six huge jars with water. When they had done this, Jesus asked them to take some of the water to the person who had organized the party.

When the man tasted the water, he was very pleased. He went to the bridegroom and told him that he had saved the very best wine till the end of the party!

The man didn't know where the wine had come from. But the servants did! Jesus had turned the water into wine.

Look and see where the water jars are.

JESUS TEACHES THE PEOPLE

Jesus told people wonderful stories about God. He helped them see how much God loved them and how he cared about everything that worried them.

"God blesses people who love him," Jesus told them. "They are special to him. God blesses people who are sad and cares for them. God blesses people who don't show off, and who try hard to do as he says. God blesses people who are kind to others and who help them make friends.

"God wants you to be kind to other people even if they are unkind to you. And God wants you to tell him about all the things that worry you. He looks after the birds that fly above you and makes sure they have enough to eat. And he makes the flowers in the meadows beautiful. God loves you even more than the birds and the flowers and so will make sure you have everything you need."

Look and see the bird Jesus was talking about.

JESUS SAYS TO BE KIND

Jesus taught his friends to be kind to other people, to think kind thoughts about them, and to speak kind words about them.

"It's easy to look at others and see only the bad things about them, or listen to nasty things other people say about them.

"Try not to do that. No one is perfect. Everyone you know does things that are naughty. Some people do it in public and everyone knows about it. Other people do bad things in secret. And you do things that are wrong too.

"God knows all about you and the people around you. Tell him you are sorry for the things you do that are wrong or that hurt other people. And let other people do the same. That way God can forgive you and you can be his friend."

Look and see a prisoner in chains.

JESUS HEALS A MAN'S HAND

Every Sabbath day, all the people rested. It
was the law that they could not work at all.
Instead they prayed, they learned about God,
and they told him how much they loved him.

One Sabbath Jesus saw a man with a hand
that was badly hurt.

There were some men who didn't like what
Jesus taught the people about God. They
tried to trick him.

"Would it be wrong to heal this man on the
Sabbath?" they asked Jesus. But Jesus
answered them with another question.

"If your sheep fell into a ditch on the
Sabbath day, wouldn't you pull it out? Surely it
is right to do good things on the Sabbath
day?"

Then Jesus asked the man with the injured
hand to stretch it out.

Jesus healed his hand so that it was like new.

But the men who had tried to trick Jesus
didn't like it at all. They began to plot against
him and to find a way to kill him.

Look and see how many leaders look mad at
Jesus.

A ROMAN OFFICER COMES TO JESUS

One day Jesus visited Capernaum, by Lake Galilee.

In the town there was a Roman officer who had helped the people and had always been good to them. Now the officer's servant was very ill and they thought he would die.

The Roman officer knew that Jesus could heal people. So he asked if Jesus would make his servant well. Jesus was happy to help. He offered to go to the officer's house.

The officer shook his head.

"You don't need to come to my house," he said. "I know if you simply say he will be well, then he will not die. Just give the order."

Jesus was amazed. He hadn't met anyone yet who trusted him in the way the Roman officer did. So Jesus gave the order.

And when the officer got home, he found his servant was well again.

Look and see why the child is chasing the dog.

THE TERRIBLE STORM

Jesus was tired after a very busy day.

He asked his friends to take him across to the other side of Lake Galilee. Once he had sat down to rest in the little boat, he quickly fell asleep.

Before long the clouds moved across the sky. The wind started to fill the sails and the waves tossed the boat up and down, up and down. Then lightning flashed and thunder rolled. A storm had blown up on the lake!

The disciples were frightened.

"Save us, Jesus!" they shouted.

But Jesus was fast asleep!

"Save us or we'll drown!" they called again.

This time Jesus heard them. He stood up and spoke to the wind and waves. And just as suddenly as it had started, the wind dropped and the waves were still.

The disciples stared at their friend and teacher. They were amazed. Who could he be if even the wind and waves obeyed him?

Look and see four reasons why the disciples were frightened.

66

THE WOMAN IN THE CROWD

Some time later, a man came to Jesus and begged for help. The man's name was Jairus and Jesus agreed to go with him. As Jesus moved through the crowd of people, he felt someone touch his cloak.

"Who touched me?" Jesus asked.

"What do you mean?" the disciples asked. "Surely any one of these people could have touched you."

But Jesus knew that someone who was ill had touched him, and in doing so, they had been healed. He looked around.

Then a woman stepped forward.

"It was me," she said, anxious that Jesus would be angry. She knelt at his feet.

"I have been ill for twelve years," she said. "I have spent everything I have on doctors to make me well, but no cure has worked. I thought if I just touched your cloak, I might be healed."

Jesus was not angry. He smiled.

"You believed I could help you, and now you are well. Go home now."

Look and see the woman who touched Jesus.

JAIRUS'S DAUGHTER

While Jesus was helping the woman in the crowd, a servant came running from the house of Jairus.

Jairus's little daughter was very ill, and he wanted Jesus to help her.

"It's too late now," the servant said. "Jairus's daughter has died!"

Jairus wanted to cry! If only Jesus hadn't stopped to help someone else!

"Don't worry," said Jesus to Jairus. "Trust me and she will be well."

Jesus made his way to the man's house and went in with three of his friends.

"Your little girl is just sleeping," he said.

Jesus took the girl by the hand.

"Get up, little girl," he said to her.

The girl opened her eyes. She looked at Jesus and smiled. She looked at her mother and father who were amazed!

"Now give her something to eat," said Jesus. "She's hungry."

Jairus and the girl's mother were overjoyed.

Look and see how many of Jesus' friends were with him in the room.

THE STORY OF THE GOOD SAMARITAN

A man once came to Jesus and asked him a question.

"Who is *my* neighbor?"

To answer the man, Jesus told a story.

"A man was traveling along the lonely road from Jerusalem to Jericho," Jesus said. "Suddenly, he met a gang of robbers. They took the man's money, stole his clothes, and hurt him badly.

"A priest was traveling along the same road. But the priest pretended he hadn't seen the man. He walked on by.

"Later, a temple helper walked past. The man looked the other way and didn't stop.

"But then a Samaritan came by. He stopped, bathed the man's wounds, and took him to an inn. He gave the innkeeper money and asked him to look after the man until he was better."

Jesus turned to the man who asked the question.

"Who was the man's neighbor?" Jesus asked.

"The one who helped him," replied the man.

Look and see what animal the Samaritan used to take the man to the inn.

FOOD FOR HUNGRY PEOPLE

People followed Jesus wherever he went. They listened to his stories and asked him to heal them.

One day they had been with him on a hillside for a long time and Jesus saw that they were hungry. He asked his friends where they could get food to share with them.

Philip was amazed. There were thousands of men, women, and children!

But Andrew brought a boy to Jesus.

"This boy has five small loaves of bread and two fish..."

Jesus asked his friends to get the people to sit down. Then he took the boy's food. He thanked God for it and handed it out.

Everyone had enough and no one was hungry. The disciples then gathered up what was left and filled twelve baskets! Five thousand people had been fed. It was a miracle.

Look and see who brought their loaves and fish to Jesus.

THE STORY OF THE LOST SHEEP

Jesus often told the people stories about how much God loved them. Once he told a story about a shepherd who had a hundred sheep.

"One day when the shepherd was counting his sheep, he found that one was missing," said Jesus.

"The shepherd made sure the other ninety-nine sheep were safely in their field, and then he went to look for the sheep that was lost.

"The shepherd looked everywhere until he found the one lost sheep. Then he picked it up and carried it home on his shoulders.

"The shepherd was so happy that he arranged a party for all his friends!

"God is like that shepherd," said Jesus.

"He loves all the people he has made. He looks after all those who stay close beside him, following his ways. But if any stray away and get lost, he can't be happy until they are safe again."

Look and see why the lost sheep was in danger.

THE LOVING FATHER

Once Jesus told a story about a man with two sons. The younger son wanted to leave home.

His father gave him money, but he was very sad that his son wanted to go away.

The son had many friends while he had lots of money. But when he had spent everything, all his friends left him.

He had to get a job feeding pigs. Then he realized how silly he was. His father's servants had more to eat than he did, and he didn't even like pigs! So he decided to go home, say he was sorry, and ask for a job on his father's farm.

But when he got near to the house, he saw his father had been waiting for him. His father was so happy to see him, he gave him clean, new clothes and held a party for him.

Jesus wanted people to know that God was just like that father. He loves his children very much.

Look and see how many pigs you can count.

THE BLIND BEGGAR

Bartimaeus was a blind man. He couldn't work. He couldn't earn money. So he sat day by day by the side of the road, hoping people would throw a coin into his bowl so he could buy food to eat.

One day he heard the sound of many people coming along the road. He knew someone important must be there. Then he heard someone say it was Jesus.

Bartimaeus had heard about Jesus. He knew that he made people well. He also knew he was kind and would help him!

"Help me!" he shouted. "Help me, Jesus!"

The people frowned at Bartimaeus. They thought Jesus had more important things to do.

But Jesus stopped to talk to him.

"How can I help?" Jesus asked him.

"I want to see!" he answered.

So Jesus made Bartimaeus well. He was so happy he threw away his begging bowl and stick and followed Jesus.

Look and see Bartimaeus' begging bowl and stick.

THE MAN WHO CLIMBED A TREE

Like everyone else, Zacchaeus wanted to see Jesus when he came to Jericho.

But Zacchaeus was not very tall. When a crowd gathered, he couldn't see over their heads! And although Zacchaeus had lots of money, he didn't have any friends. No one would let him through.

So Zacchaeus climbed into the branches of a fig tree. From there he could see Jesus coming closer...and closer...and closer.

"Come down here!" Jesus said, looking up at him. "I must come to your house today."

Zacchaeus couldn't believe it. Why would Jesus want to be his friend? But Zacchaeus scrambled down the tree and took Jesus to his home.

The crowd wasn't happy; Zacchaeus was rich because he had cheated people. But after being with Jesus, Zacchaeus decided to give even more money back than he had stolen from people. He shared all he had with the poor.

Zacchaeus was a changed person because of Jesus!

Look and see Zacchaeus.

JESUS RIDES A DONKEY

Jesus and his friends went to Jerusalem for the special Passover feast.

Jesus had asked his friends to find him a donkey to ride on. So Jesus came into the city on the donkey's back.

There were many people following Jesus. Others were waiting for him and saw him coming.

Some of them were people Jesus had helped. Others knew people Jesus had made well. Many had heard the wonderful stories Jesus had told about God or they had seen the amazing things he had done.

The people cheered and waved huge palm branches. They threw down their cloaks in front of the donkey to make a path.

"Hosanna!" they shouted. "Here comes Jesus the king!"

Look and see the cloaks on the path.

FRIENDS AND ENEMIES

Jesus planned to eat the Passover meal with his friends.

Before the meal, Jesus washed their feet.

"Care for each other as I have cared for you," he told them. "This is how other people will know that you are my followers and that you love God."

Then they sat down together and ate the special meal of lamb and herbs, bread and wine. But Jesus was sad. He knew that soon he would be taken from his friends.

Jesus took the bread, thanked God, and broke it into pieces. He shared it with his friends.

"This is my body," he said. Then Jesus took the wine.

"This is my blood," he said.

During the meal, Judas Iscariot, one of the disciples, left the room quietly to tell the guards how to capture Jesus. He had decided to betray his friend for thirty pieces of silver.

Look and see how many friends are eating with Jesus.

A HORRIBLE DEATH

The guards arrested Jesus later on Passover night. They brought him before the Roman governor, Pontius Pilate.

The crowd outside was full of people who were jealous because Jesus was so popular.

"Crucify him!" the crowd shouted, again and again. So Jesus was forced to carry a cross to a hillside outside the city walls.

He had provided food for hungry people. He had calmed a storm and helped the blind see again. Many people who had been ill were made well. And he had told everyone about how much God loved them.

But he was nailed to a cross between two thieves.

Jesus' friends and his mother watched, weeping, until Jesus cried out to God in a loud voice just before he died.

Some of his friends took the body of Jesus down from the cross and buried him in a rock tomb. Then they rolled a big stone across the entrance.

Look and see how many crosses there are.

THE STONE IS ROLLED AWAY

Very early on Sunday morning, Mary Magdalene went to the tomb where they had buried Jesus. She was very sad.

She came with herbs and spices so she could anoint the body of Jesus. There had not been time to do this earlier because his body had to be buried quickly before the special Sabbath day.

But when she got there, the big stone had already been rolled away. The tomb was empty! Where could Jesus be?

Then Mary was startled by two angels!

"Jesus is alive!" they told her. "Go and tell everyone!"

Mary didn't know what to think! But she ran as fast as she could until she found Jesus' friends. Then she told them the news.

"Jesus is alive!" she shouted. And they went to the garden where the empty tomb was to see for themselves. Jesus had died, but God had raised him to new life.

Look and see how many angels are by the tomb.

THE LAKESIDE BREAKFAST

Some days had passed since Mary had seen the empty tomb. Since then all the disciples had seen Jesus alive again.

Now, some of the disciples were out fishing on Lake Galilee. It had not been a good night. They had caught no fish at all.

As the sun rose, a man called to them from the shore.

"Throw your nets out on the other side!"

The disciples were tired, but they did as he suggested. And to their surprise, their nets nearly broke with the weight of all the fish!

"Can it be Jesus?" John asked.

Peter jumped into the water and swam to the shore.

There he found Jesus cooking bread and fish for all of them. Jesus had died but he was really alive again. He told them that soon he would return to be with God in Heaven, but he would send the Holy Spirit so that they would never be alone again.

Look and see what time of day it is.

WHERE TO FIND THE BIBLE STORIES:

A beautiful world, Genesis 1:1-31

Noah and the great flood, Genesis 6:1 – 8:22

God makes a promise, Genesis 13:16; 15:5; 21:1-7

A special wife for Isaac, Genesis 24:1-67

The brothers who quarreled, Genesis 27:1-45

The favorite son, Genesis 37:1-36; 39:1-5; 42:1 – 45:7

The princess and the baby, Exodus 2:1-10

The walls that tumbled down, Joshua 6:2-20

Deborah leads her people, Judges 4:4 – 5:31

Gideon trusts God, Judges 7:15-21

Samson, the strong man, Judges 14:5-6; 16:4-30

The boy who listened, 1 Samuel 3:1-10

Saul and the missing donkeys, 1 Samuel 9:1 – 10:1

David, the giant-killer, 1 Samuel 17:12-51

Solomon, the wise king, 1 Kings 3:5-28

Elijah runs from King Ahab, 1 Kings 17:1-16; 18:15-45

Naaman washes in the river, 2 Kings 5:1-14

The angel of death, 2 Chronicles 32:1-22

Jonah runs from God, Jonah 1:1 – 3:10

Daniel is thrown to the lions, Daniel 6:1-28

Nehemiah rebuilds the walls, Nehemiah 1:1 – 6:16; 8:1-18

Esther saves her people, Esther 2:5 – 7:10

The baby in the manger, Luke 2:1-20

John baptizes Jesus, Luke 3:1-6, 18, 21-22

Following Jesus, Matthew 4:18-22; Mark 3:14-19

Jesus goes to a wedding, John 2:1-11

Jesus teaches the people, Matthew 5:1-9; 6:25-34

Jesus says to be kind, Matthew 7:1-5

Jesus heals a man's hand, Matthew 12:9-13

A Roman officer comes to Jesus, Luke 7:1-10

The terrible storm, Luke 8:22-25

The woman in the crowd, Luke 8:40-48

Jairus's daughter, Luke 8:49-56

The story of the good Samaritan, Luke 10:25-37

Food for hungry people, John 6:1-13

The story of the lost sheep, Luke 15:3-7

The loving father, Luke 15:11-32

The blind beggar, Mark 10:46-52

The man who climbed a tree, Luke 19:1-10

Jesus rides a donkey, Luke 19:28-38

Friends and enemies, Matthew 26:14-16, 20-28

A horrible death, Luke 23:26-53

The stone is rolled away, Luke 24:1-8

The lakeside breakfast, John 21:1-14